play *guitar* with..
modern rock

HAL LEONARD EUROPE

Distributed by Music Sales Limited

Published by
Hal Leonard Europe
A Music Sales/Hal Leonard Joint Venture Company
14-15 Berners Street, London W1T 3LJ, UK.

Exclusive Distributors:
MUSIC SALES LIMITED
Distribution Centre, Newmarket Road,
Bury St Edmunds, Suffolk IP33 3YB, UK.

Order No. HLE90004486
ISBN 978-1-78038-381-1
This book © Copyright 2012 Hal Leonard Europe.

Printed in the EU

www.musicsales.com

Edited by Adrian Hopkins
Cover designed by Liz Barrand

Charlie Brown
Cousins
Days Are Forgotten
I Bet You Look Good On The Dancefloor
Rope
Guitars: Arthur Dick
Bass guitar: Paul Townsend
Drums: Noam Lederman

Mr. Brightside
Guitars, Bass guitar, Keyboards: Tom Fleming
Drums: Dave Cottrell

Pyro
Tracking, mixing, and mastering by
Jake Johnson & Bill Maynard at Paradyme Productions
Guitars by Doug Boduch
Bass by Tom McGirr
Keyboards by Warren Wiegratz
Drums by Scott Schroedl

CD recorded and mixed by Jonas Persson

guitar tablature explained

Guitar music can be explained in three different ways: on a musical stave, in tablature, and in rhythm slashes.

RHYTHM SLASHES: are written above the stave. Strum chords in the rhythm indicated. Round noteheads indicate single notes.

THE MUSICAL STAVE: shows pitches and rhythms and is divided by lines into bars. Pitches are named after the first seven letters of the alphabet.

TABLATURE: graphically represents the guitar fingerboard. Each horizontal line represents a string, and each number represents a fret.

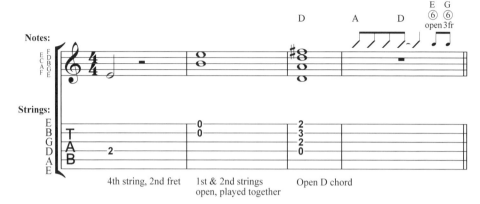

4th string, 2nd fret   1st & 2nd strings open, played together   Open D chord

definitions for special guitar notation

SEMI-TONE BEND: Strike the note and bend up a semi-tone (½ step).

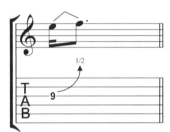

WHOLE-TONE BEND: Strike the note and bend up a whole-tone (full step).

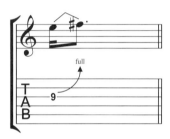

GRACE NOTE BEND: Strike the note and bend as indicated. Play the first note as quickly as possible.

QUARTER-TONE BEND: Strike the note and bend up a ¼ step

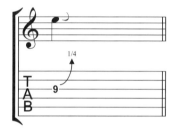

BEND & RELEASE: Strike the note and bend up as indicated, then release back to the original note.

COMPOUND BEND & RELEASE: Strike the note and bend up and down in the rhythm indicated.

PRE-BEND: Bend the note as indicated, then strike it.

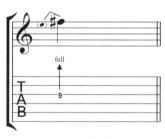

PRE-BEND & RELEASE: Bend the note as indicated. Strike it and release the note back to the original pitch.

HAMMER-ON: Strike the first note with one finger, then sound the second note (on the same string) with another finger by fretting it without picking.

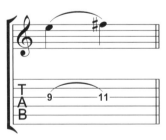

PULL-OFF: Place both fingers on the note to be sounded, strike the first note and without picking, pull the finger off to sound the second note.

LEGATO SLIDE (GLISS): Strike the first note and then slide the same fret-hand finger up or down to the second note. The second note is not struck.

MUFFLED STRINGS: A percussive sound is produced by laying the first hand across the string(s) without depressing, and striking them with the pick hand.

NATURAL HARMONIC: Strike the note while the fret-hand lightly touches the string directly over the fret indicated.

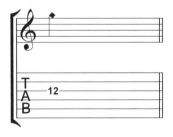

PICK SCRAPE: The edge of the pick is rubbed down (or up) the string, producing a scratchy sound.

PALM MUTING: The note is partially muted by the pick hand lightly touching the string(s) just before the bridge.

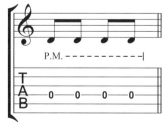

SHIFT SLIDE (GLISS & RESTRIKE) Same as legato slide, except the second note is struck.

TAP HARMONIC: The note is fretted normally and a harmonic is produced by tapping or slapping the fret indicated in brackets (which will be twelve frets higher than the fretted note.)

TAPPING: Hammer ('tap') the fret indicated with the pick-hand index or middle finger and pull-off to the note fretted by the fret hand.

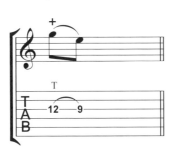

PINCH HARMONIC: The note is fretted normally and a harmonic is produced by adding the edge of the thumb or the tip of the index finger of the pick hand to the normal pick attack.

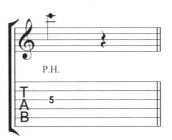

ARTIFICIAL HARMONIC: The note fretted normally and a harmonic is produced by gently resting the pick hand's index finger directly above the indicated fret (in brackets) while plucking the appropriate string.

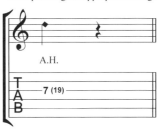

TRILL: Very rapidly alternate between the notes indicated by continuously hammering-on and pulling-off.

RAKE: Drag the pick across the strings with a single motion.

TREMOLO PICKING: The note is picked as rapidly and continuously as possible.

ARPEGGIATE: Play the notes of the chord indicated by quickly rolling them from bottom to top.

SWEEP PICKING: Rhythmic downstroke and/or upstroke motion across the strings.

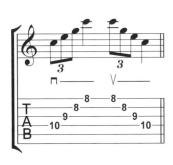

VIBRATO DIVE BAR AND RETURN: The pitch of the note or chord is dropped a specific number of steps (in rhythm) then returned to the original pitch.

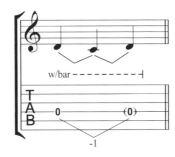

VIBRATO BAR SCOOP: Depress the bar just before striking the note, then quickly release the bar.

VIBRATO BAR DIP: Strike the note and then immediately drop a specific number of steps, then release back to the original pitch.

additional musical definitions

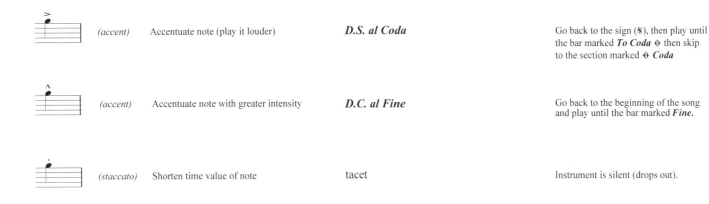

	(accent)	Accentuate note (play it louder)	***D.S. al Coda***	Go back to the sign (𝄋), then play until the bar marked ***To Coda*** ⊕ then skip to the section marked ⊕ ***Coda***
(accent)	Accentuate note with greater intensity	***D.C. al Fine***	Go back to the beginning of the song and play until the bar marked ***Fine.***
(staccato)	Shorten time value of note	tacet	Instrument is silent (drops out).

Downstroke

Upstroke

Repeat bars between signs

NOTE: Tablature numbers in brackets mean:
1. The note is sustained, but a new articulation (such as hammer-on or slide) begins
2. A note may be fretted but not necessarily played.

When a repeat section has different endings, play the first ending only the first time and the second ending only the second time.

charlie brown

Words and Music by
Chris Martin, Guy Berryman, Jon Buckland, Will Champion & Brian Eno

Full performance demo: track 1
Backing only: track 8

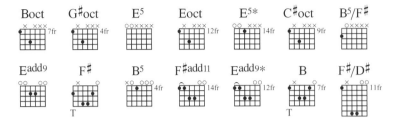

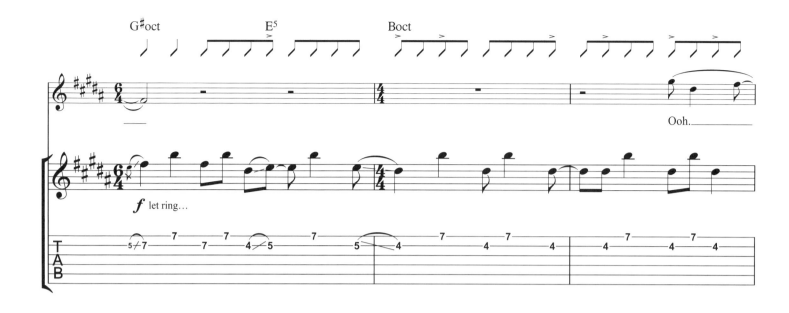

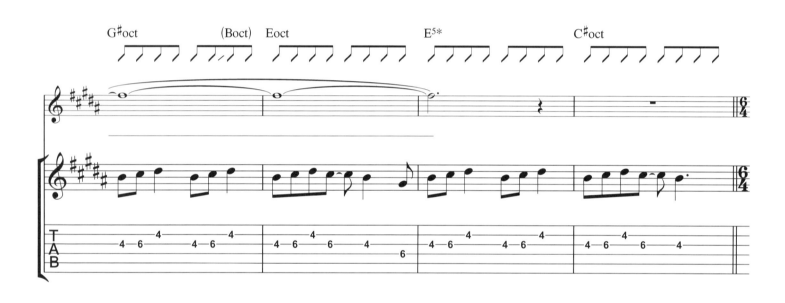

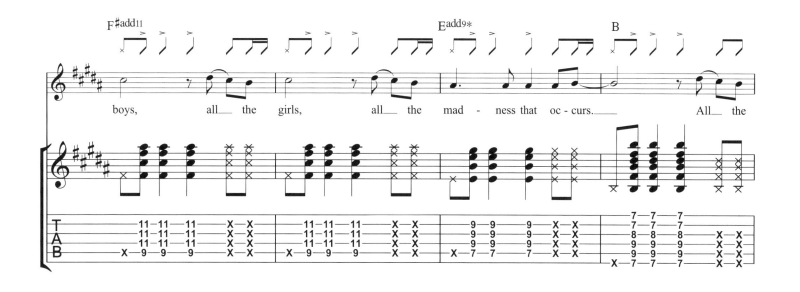

boys, all the girls, all the mad - ness that oc - curs.___ All the

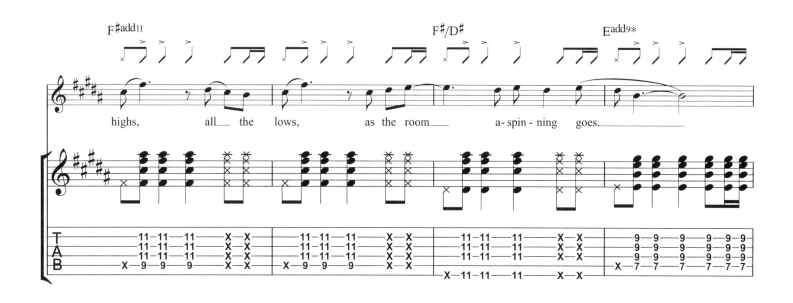

highs, all the lows, as the room___ a- spin - ning goes.___

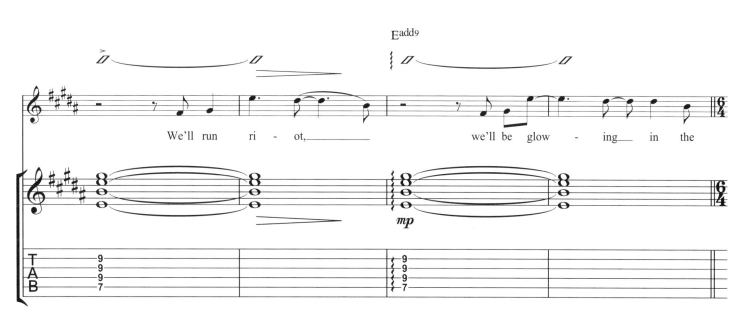

We'll run ri - ot,___ we'll be glow - ing in the

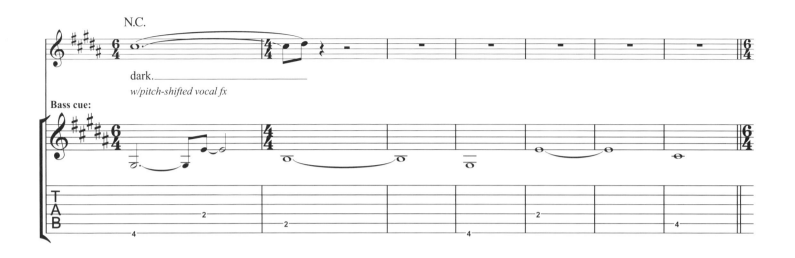

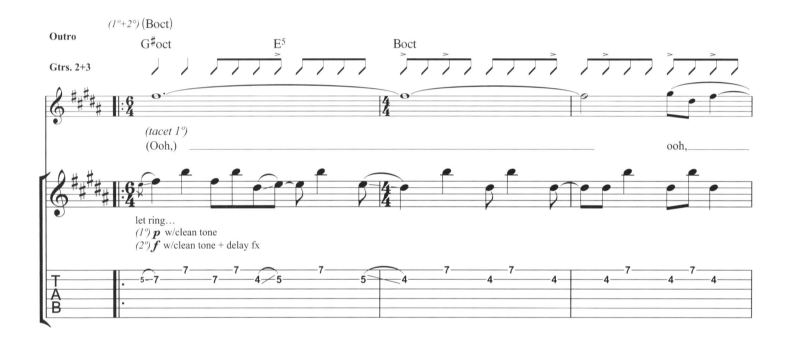

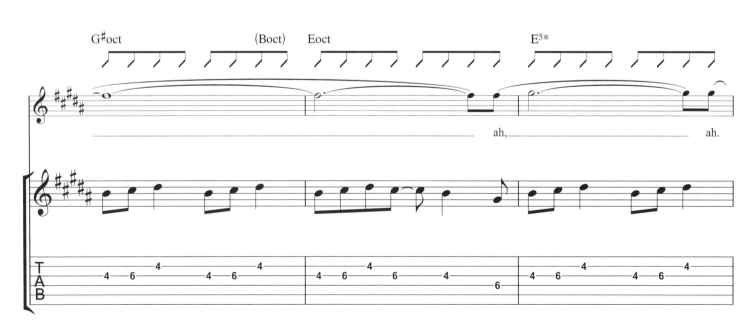

2. Ooh, ___ So we'll soar ___

lu - mi - nous and wir-

- ed, ___ we'll be glow - ing in the dark. ___

cousins

Words by Ezra Koenig

Music by Chris Baio, Rostam Batmanglij, Ezra Koenig & Christopher Tomson

Full performance demo: track 2
Backing only: track 9

3. In - t'rest-ing col-ours I dis-cov-ered my-self.___ If your art life is grit-ty, you'll be
4. You could turn your back on the bit-ter world. You could turn your back on the

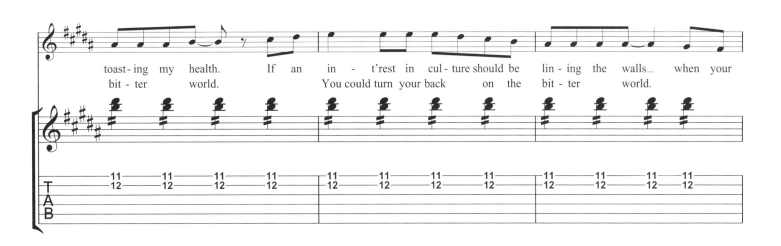

toast-ing my health. If an in - t'rest in cul-ture should be lin-ing the walls___ when your
bit-ter world. You could turn your back on the bit-ter world.

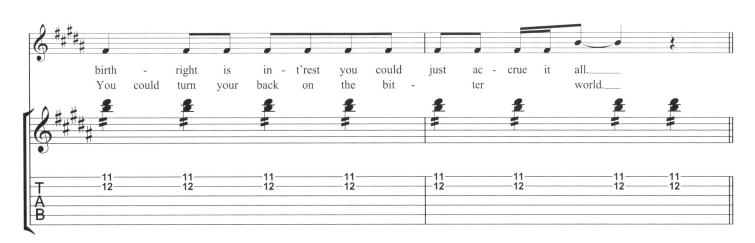

birth - right is in - t'rest you could just ac-crue it all.___
You could turn your back on the bit - ter world.___

Me and my cou - sins and you and your cou - sins, it's a line that's al - ways run - ning.

Me and my cou - sins and you and your cou - sins, I can feel it com - ing.

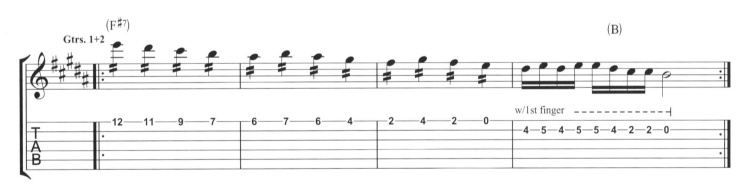

w/1st finger

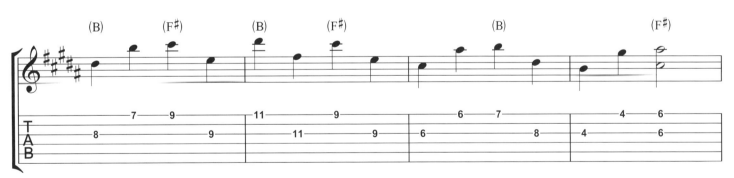

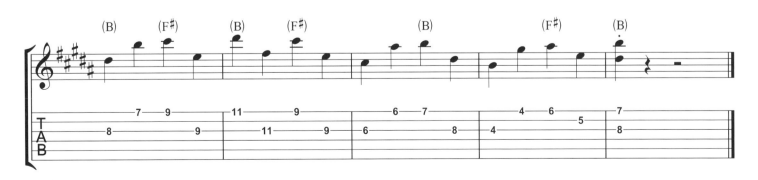

days are forgotten

Words and Music by
Words & Music by Sergio Pizzorno

Full performance demo: track 3
Backing only: track 10

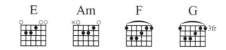

E   Am   F   G

♩ = 106

Intro
2 bar count in:

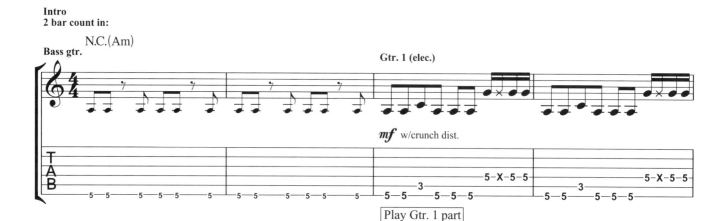

Verse

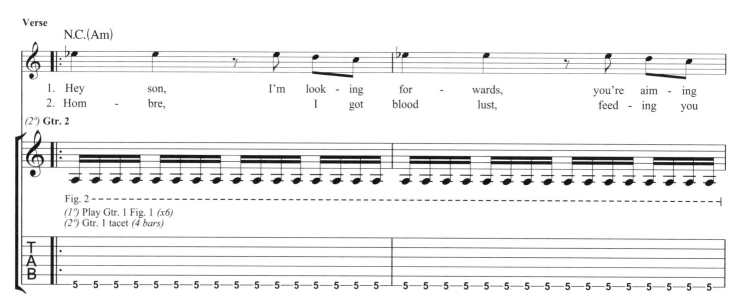

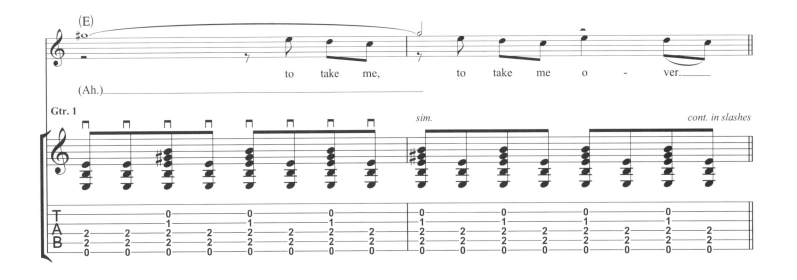

to take me, to take me o - ver.____

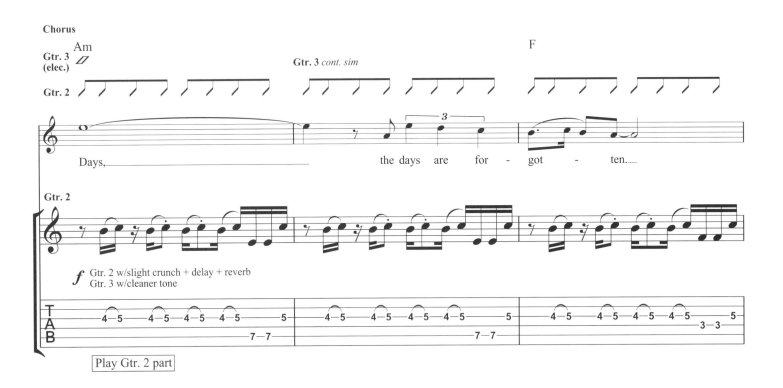

Chorus

Days,____ the days are for - got - ten.____

Gtr. 2 w/slight crunch + delay + reverb
Gtr. 3 w/cleaner tone

Play Gtr. 2 part

Now it's all o - ver,____ you've sim - ply for -

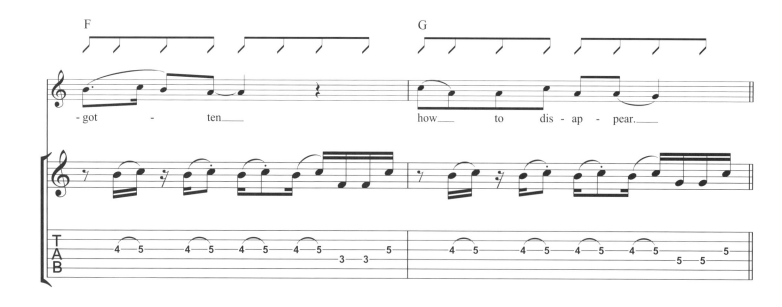

- got - ten____ how____ to dis - ap - pear.____

Bridge

I saw some - thing out there on the dark - est star.

To Coda

You were sat at home____ chew - ing on mon - key brain.____

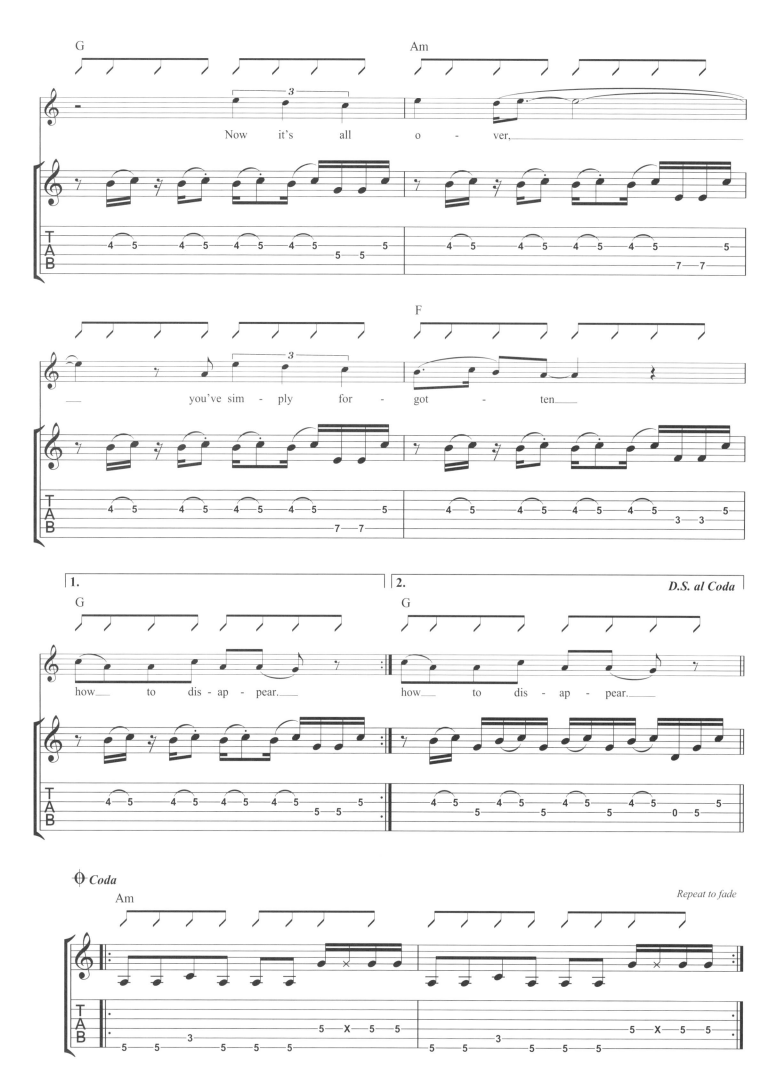

i bet you look good on the dancefloor

Words and Music by
Alexander Turner

Full performance demo: track 4
Backing only: track 11

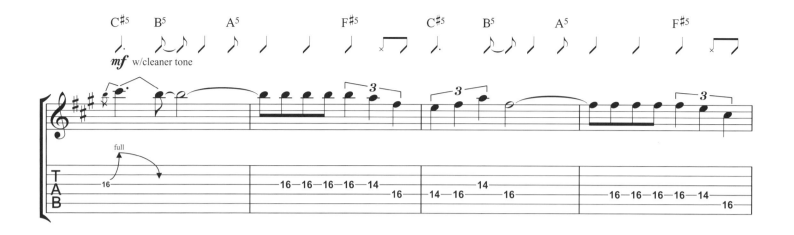

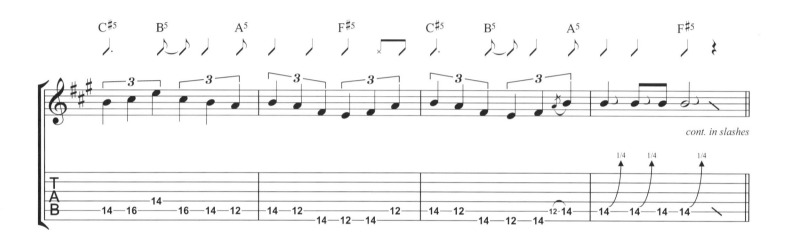

Verse
Gtrs. 1+2

1. Stop mak-ing the eyes at me, I'll stop mak-ing the eyes at____ you,____
2. I wish you'd stop ig - nor - ing me, be - cause you're send - ing me to des - pair.____

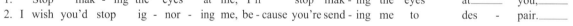

and what it is that sur - pri - ses me, is that I don't real - ly____ want you to. And your shoul - ders are
With - out a sound, yeah, you're call - ing me____ and I don't think it's____ ver - y fair that your shoul - ders are

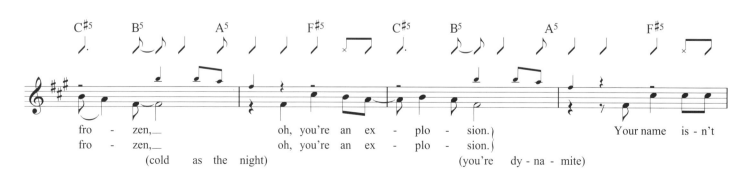

fro - zen, oh, you're an ex - plo - sion. Your name is - n't
fro - zen, oh, you're an ex - plo - sion.
(cold as the night) (you're dy - na - mite)

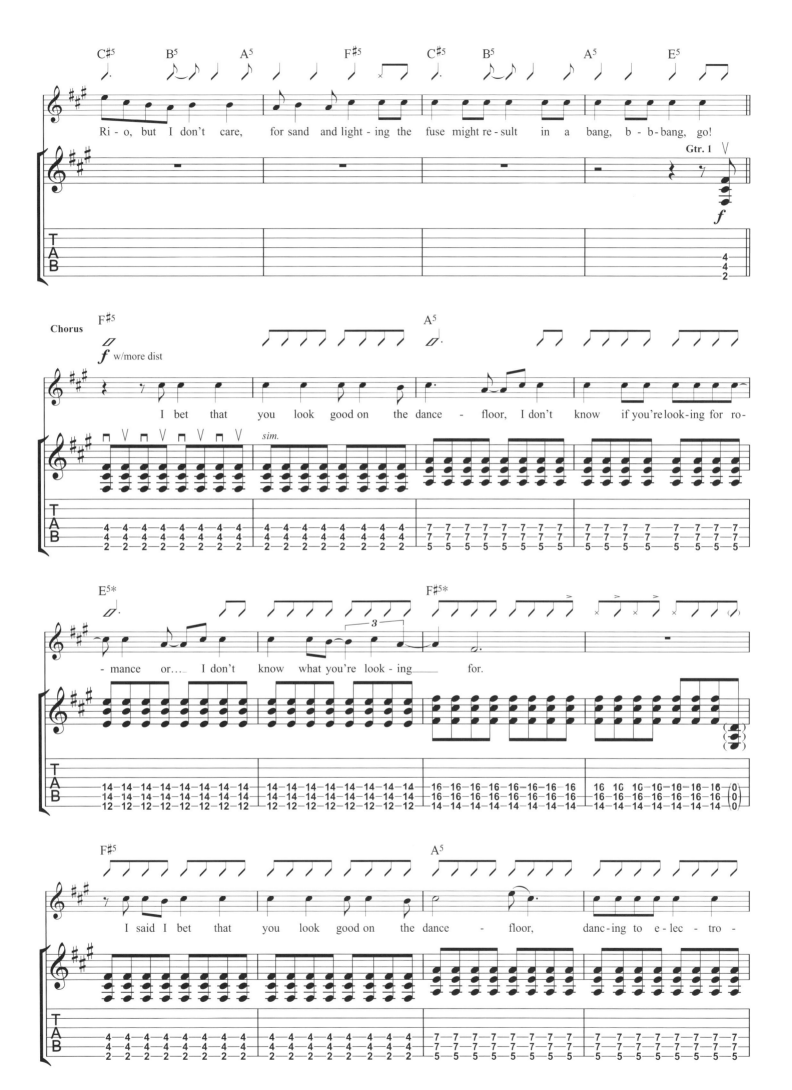

pop like a ro - bot from nine - teen eight - y - four,___ well, from nine - teen eight - y -

- four.___

- four. Oh, there in't no love___ no, no Mont - a - gues___ or Cap - u - lets,___

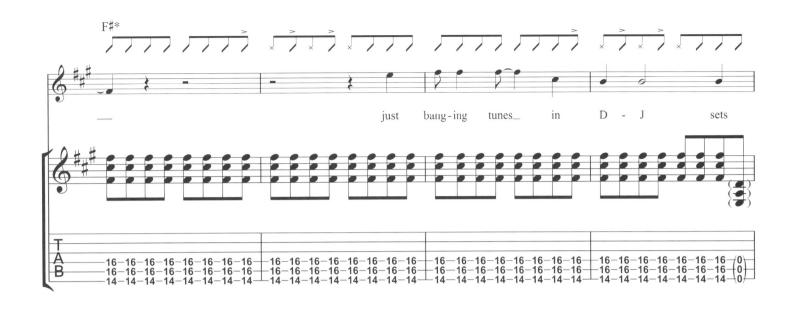

just bang-ing tunes__ in D - J sets

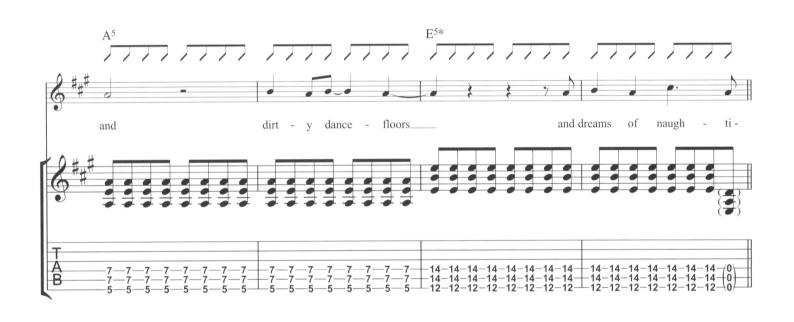

and   dirt - y dance - floors___   and dreams of naugh - ti-

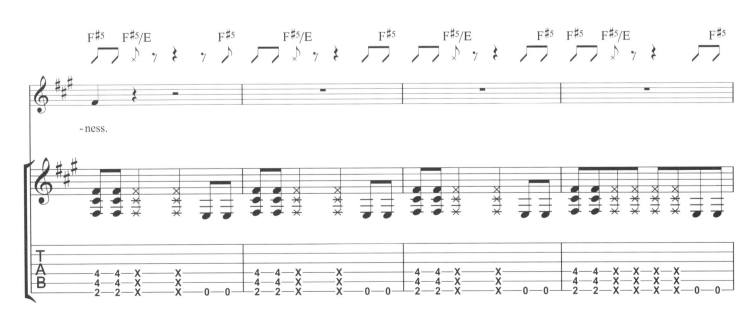

-ness.

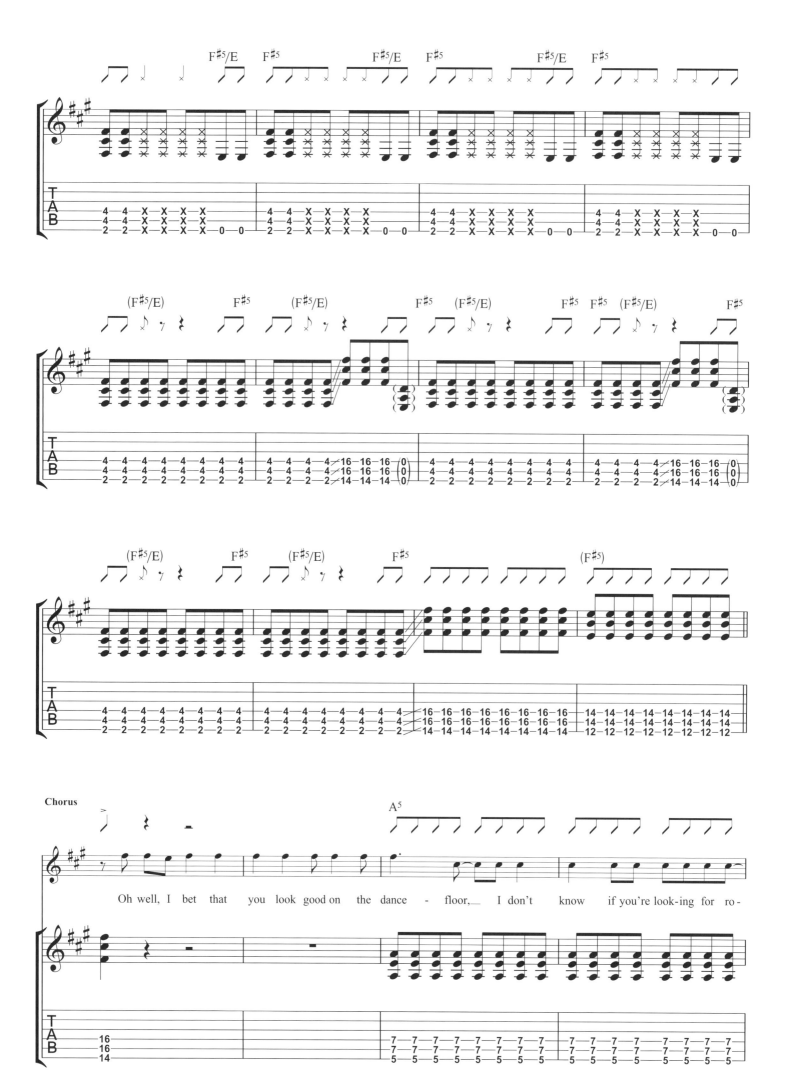

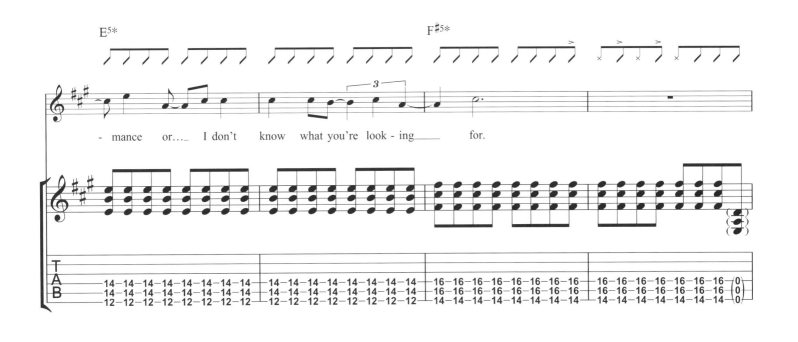

- mance or.... I don't know what you're look - ing____ for.

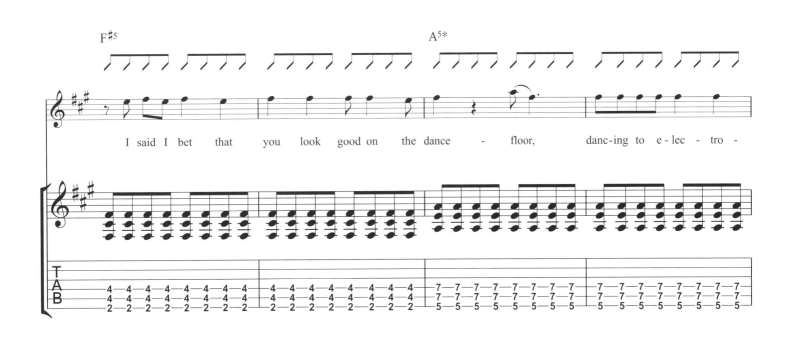

I said I bet that you look good on the dance - floor, danc-ing to e - lec - tro -

rit.

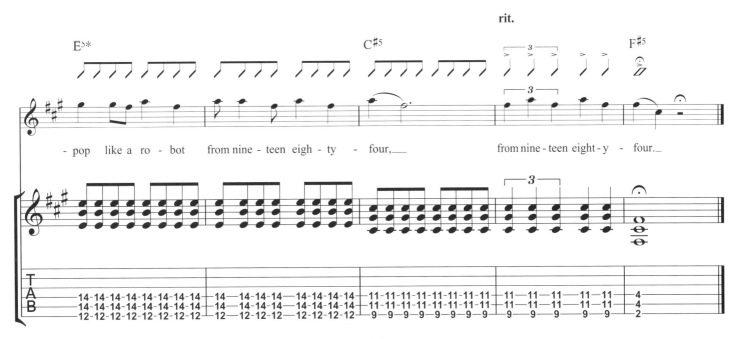

- pop like a ro - bot from nine - teen eigh - ty - four,____ from nine - teen eight - y - four.____

mr. brightside

Words and Music by
Brandon Flowers, Dave Keuning, Mark Stoermer & Ronnie Vannucci

Full performance demo: track 5
Backing only: track 12

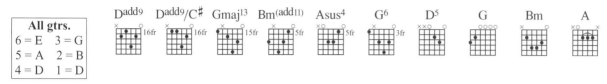

All gtrs.	
6 = E	3 = G
5 = A	2 = B
4 = D	1 = D

To match recording, tune all guitars down a semitone

Intro
2 bar count in: ♩ = 148

Gtr. 1 (elec.)

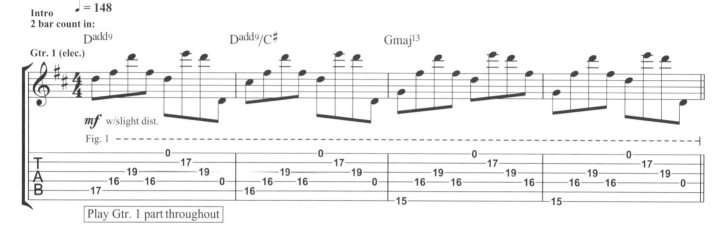

mf w/slight dist.

Fig. 1

Play Gtr. 1 part throughout

Verse

Com - ing out of my cage, ___ and I've been do - ing just fine. Got - ta, got - ta be down ___

Gtr. 1 plays Fig. 1

___ be - cause I want it all. It start - ed out with a kiss, ___ how did it end up like

this? It was on - ly a kiss, ___ it was on - ly a kiss. Now I'm fall - ing a - sleep ___

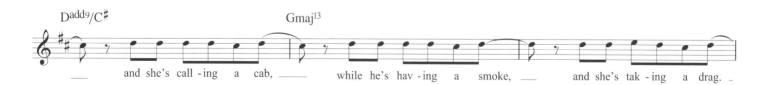

___ and she's call - ing a cab, ___ while he's hav - ing a smoke, ___ and she's tak - ing a drag. ___

___ Now they're go - ing to bed ___ and my sto - mach is sick, ___ and it's all in my head ___ but she's touch - ing his

pyro

Words and Music by
Jared Followill, Matthew Followill, Ivan Followill & Anthony Followill

Full performance demo: track 6
Backing only: track 13

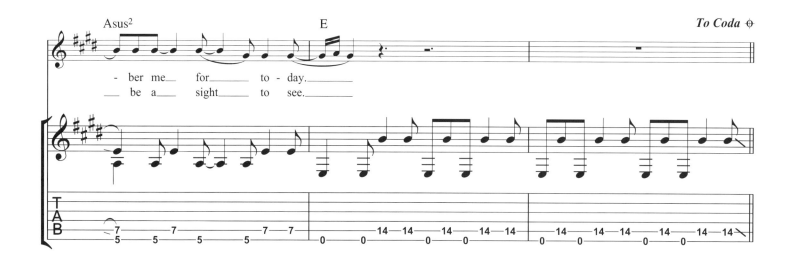

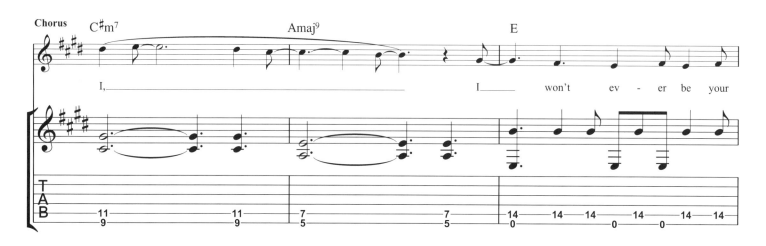

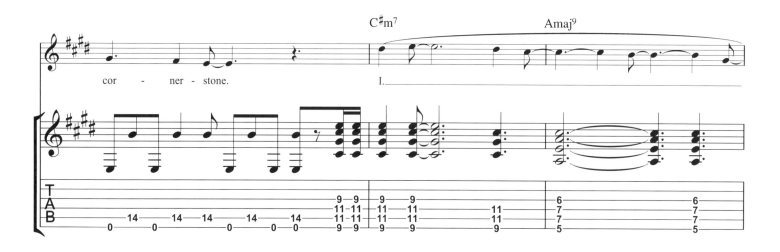

D.S. al Coda

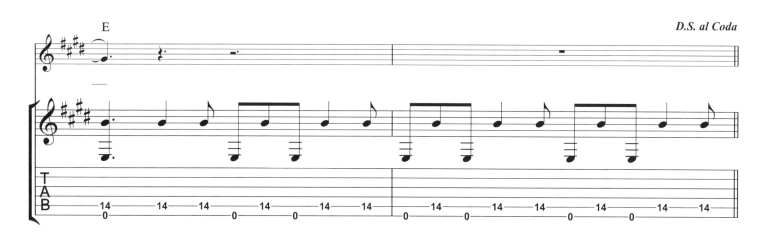

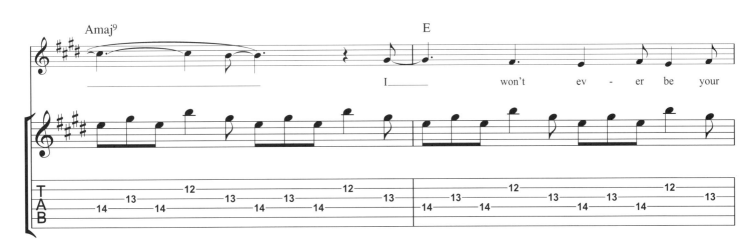

C#m7   Amaj9

cor - ner - stone.   I.

E

Guitar solo

A5   G#5   F#5

w/tremolo

A   G#m   F#m

Watch   her

tremolo off

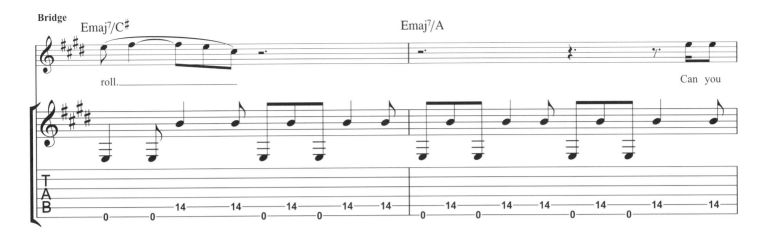

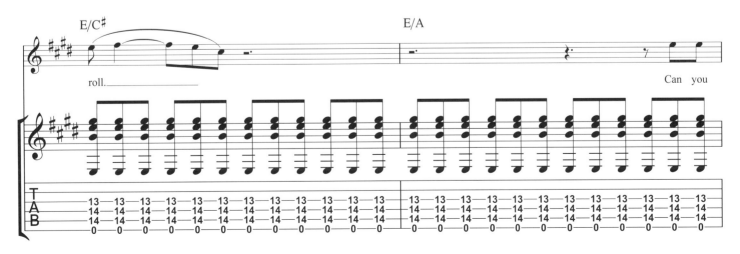

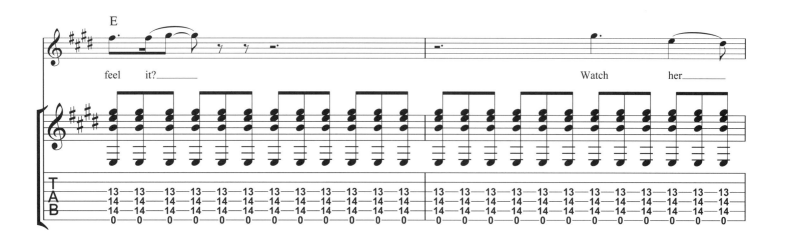

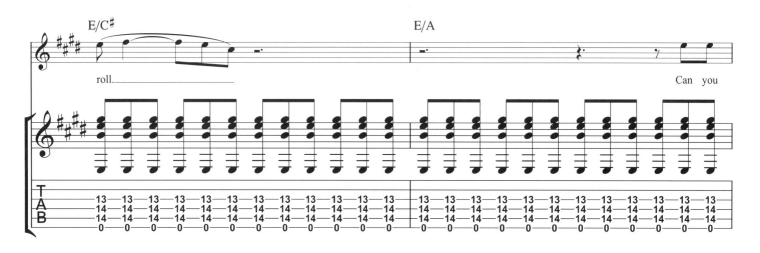

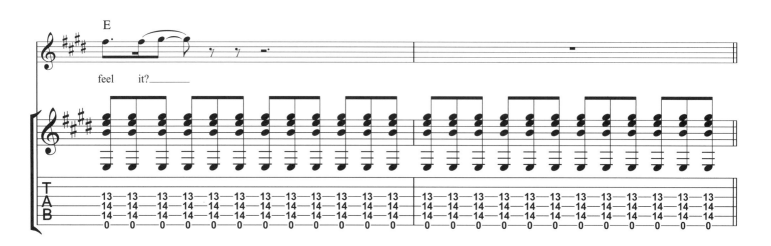

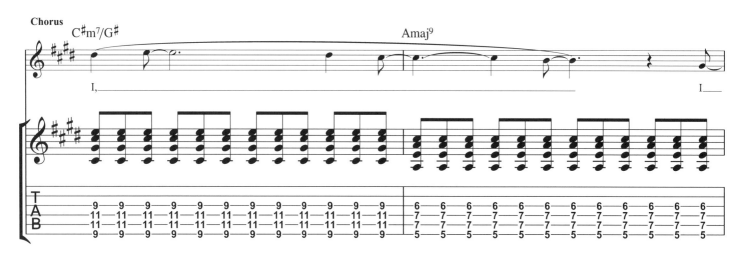

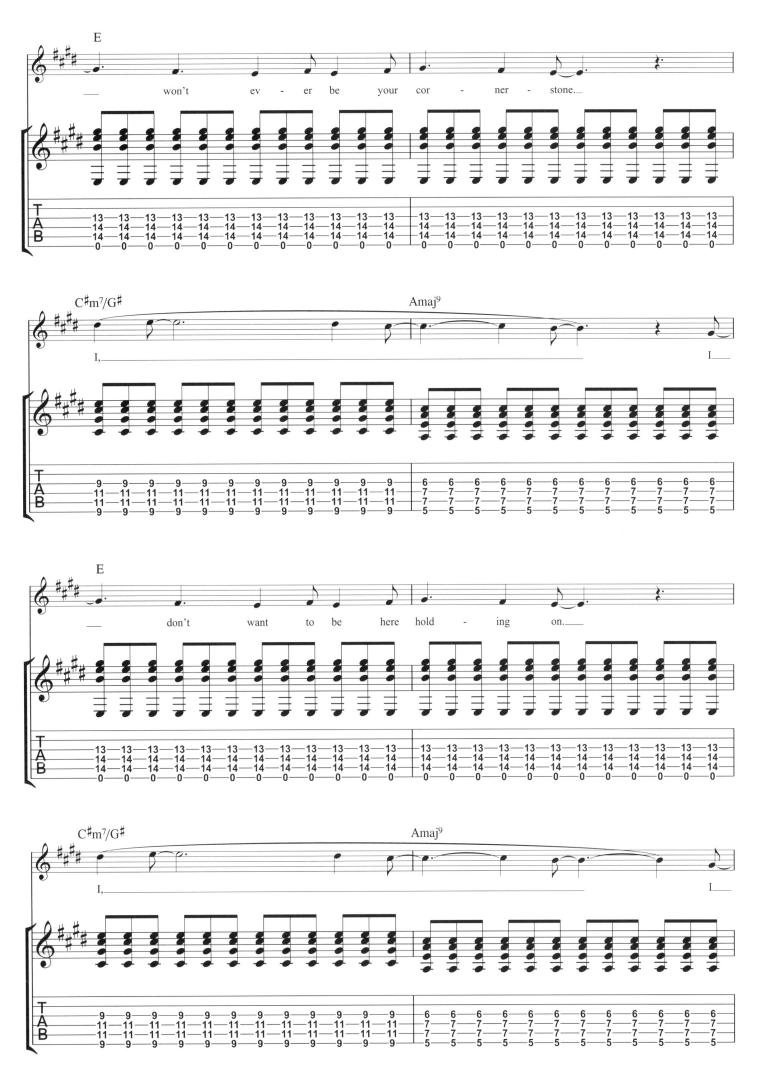

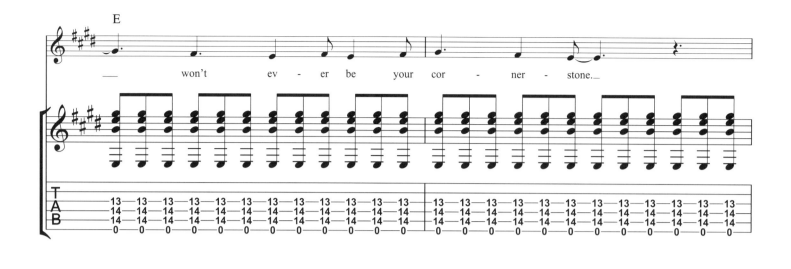

won't   ev - er be   your   cor - ner - stone.___

C#m7/G#   Amaj9   **Outro**
                                                          C#m9

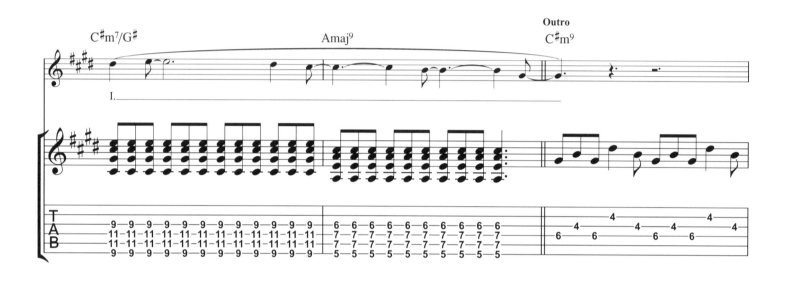

I._____

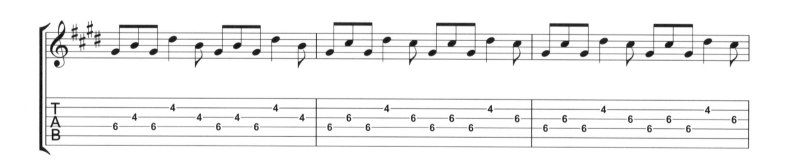

E6

rope

Words and Music by
Dave Grohl, Taylor Hawkins, Nate Mendel, Chris Shiflett & Pat Ruthensmear

Full performance demo: track 7
Backing only: track 14

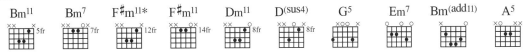

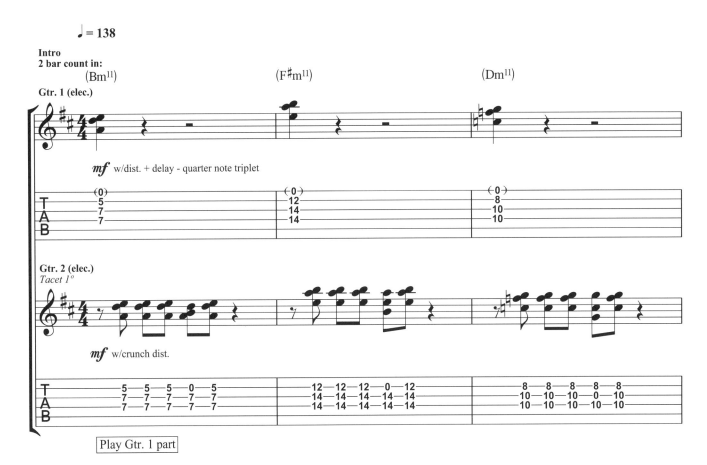

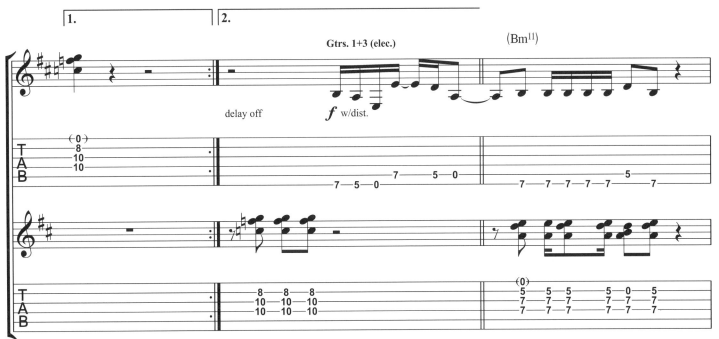

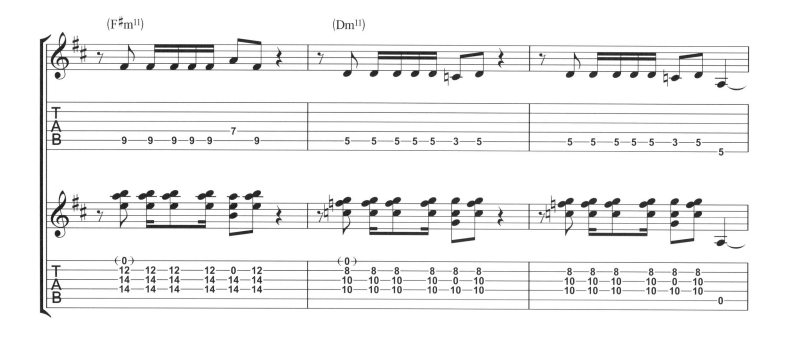

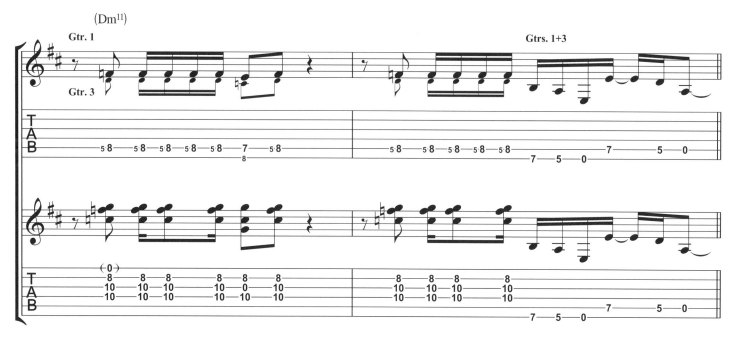

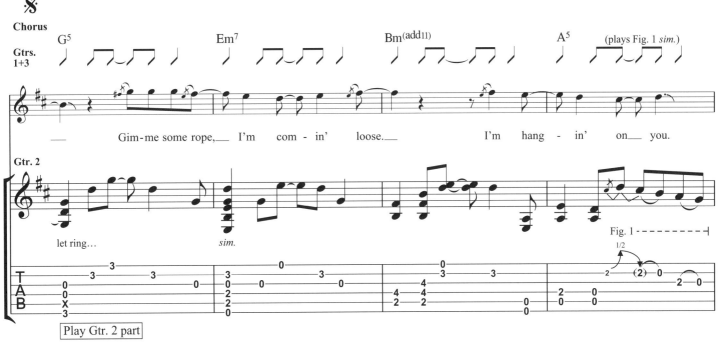

Play Gtr. 2 part

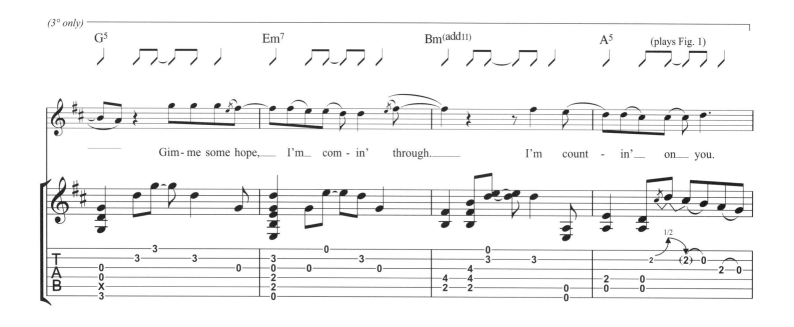

Gim-me some hope, I'm com-in' through. I'm count-in' on you.

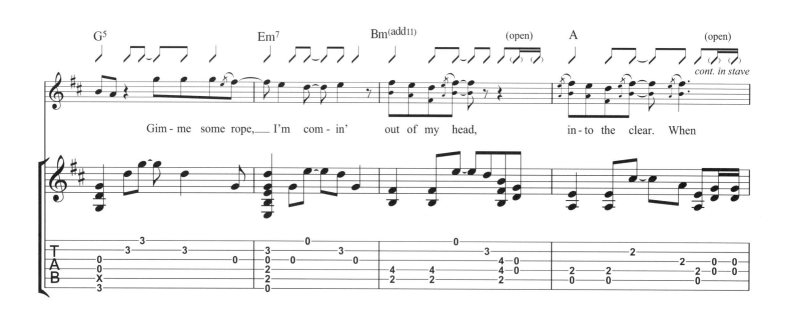

Gim-me some rope, I'm com-in' out of my head, in-to the clear. When

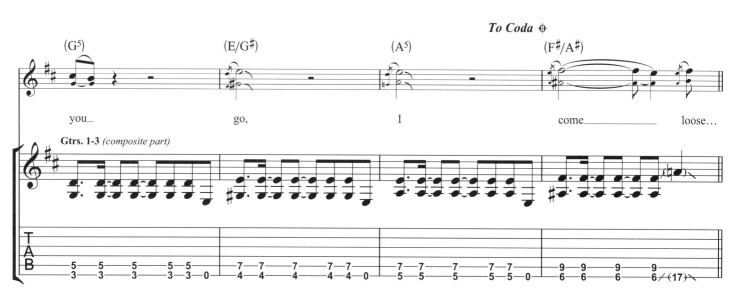

you go, I come loose...

Interlude

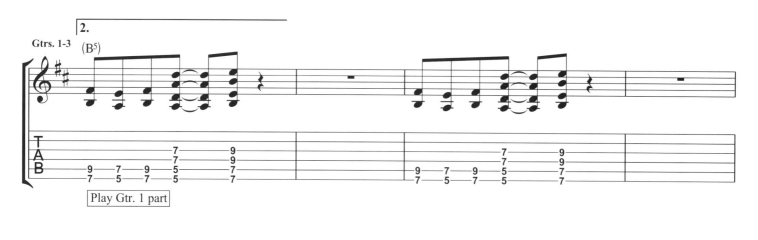

123456789

CD track listing

Full instrumental performances (with guitar)...

1 **charlie brown**
(Martin/Berryman/Buckland/Champion/Eno)
Opal Music/Universal Music Publishing MGB Limited.

2 **cousins**
(Koenig/Baio/Batmanglij/Tomson) Imagem London Limited.

3 **days are forgotten**
(Pizzorno) Sony/ATV Music Publishing (UK) Limited.

4 **i bet you look good on the dancefloor**
(Turner) EMI Music Publishing Ltd.

5 **mr brightside**
(Flowers/Keuning/Stoermer/Vannucci)
Universal Music Publishing Limited.

6 **pyro**
(Followill/Followill/Followill/Followill) Bug Music Limited.

7 **rope**
(Grohl/Hawkins/Mendel/Shiflett/Ruthensmear)
Bug Music Limited/Universal/MCA Music Limited

Backing tracks (without guitar)...

8 **charlie brown**

9 **cousins**

10 **days are forgotten**

11 **i bet you look good on the dancefloor**

12 **mr brightside**

13 **pyro**

14 **rope**

To remove your CD from the plastic sleeve, lift the small lip to break the perforation. Replace the disc after use for convenient storage.